THE BOOK OF
JONAH

"THE RUNAWAY PROPHET"

W.H. WINKLER

WESTBOW
PRESS®
A DIVISION OF THOMAS NELSON
& ZONDERVAN

WestBow Press books may be ordered through booksellers or by contacting:

WestBow Press
A Division of Thomas Nelson & Zondervan
1663 Liberty Drive
Bloomington, IN 47403
www.westbowpress.com
1 (866) 928-1240

ISBN: 978-1-9736-1192-9 (sc)
ISBN: 978-1-9736-1191-2 (hc)
ISBN: 978-1-9736-1193-6 (e)

Library of Congress Control Number: 2017919538

Print information available on the last page.

WestBow Press rev. date: 12/22/2017

DEDICATION

This book is dedicated to my wife, Judy, and to all the people who encouraged me to continue my doctoral studies. A special thank you to my brilliant professors, Dr. Herbert Leupold and Dr. Ronald Hals, who gave me a love for the Old Testament and the inspiration to go on.

TABLE OF CONTENTS

TRANSLATION FROM THE ORIGINAL HEBREW

BY
W.H. WINKLER

CHAPTER 1

1:1 Then God was speaking to Jonah, the son of Ammitai, saying:

1:2 "Arise, go to Nineveh, that great city and call out to them that their evil has come up before Me"

1:3 But Jonah rose up to run away from the face of God. He went down to Joppa and he found a ship going to Tarshish. He gave pay and he descended into it to go with them, away from the face of God.

1:4 God hurled a mighty wind into the sea and there was a great storm, so that the ship was thinking about breaking up.

1:5 Then the sailors were afraid and cried out, every man of them, to his god and they threw out the vessel's goods that were in the ship, into the sea, to lighten it. But Jonah had gone down into the inside of the ship and he had lain down and was in a heavy sleep.

1:6 So the captain approached him and spoke to him, "What do you mean, O sleeper? Arise, cry out to your God so that God will think of us, so that we do not perish."

1:7 And they said to their companions, "Come and let us cast lots, that we may perceive for whose fault this evil is upon us." So they cast lots and the lot fell upon Jonah.

1:8 Then they said to him, "Make known to us, for Whose cause this evil is upon us; What is your work? And from where do you come?

1:9 And he said to them, "I am a Hebrew; and I fear the Lord, the God of the heavens, who has made the sea and dry land."

1:10 Then the men were greatly afraid and said to him, "Why have you done this?" For the men perceived that he had fled from the face of the Lord, because he had told them this.

1:11 Then they said to him, "What shall we do to you that the sea may be quiet for us?" For the sea moved and was troubled.

1:12 And he said to them, "Lift me up and cast me away into the sea; Then shall the sea be quiet for you, for I perceive that for my sake this great storm is upon you."

1:13 Nonetheless the men rowed hard to return to the land; But they could not because the sea went against them and was stormy.

1:14 Therefore they called out to the Lord and said, "We ask you, O Lord, we ask you, do not let us perish for this man's life, and do not lay upon us innocent blood; for you, O Lord, have done as it has pleased you."

1:15 So they lifted up Jonah and hurled him into the sea; and the sea stood still from her raging.

1:16 Then the men were greatly afraid of the Lord and they offered a sacrifice to the Lord, and they made vows.

1:17 Now the Lord had assigned a great fish to swallow down Jonah. And Jonah was in the belly of the fish three days and three nights.

CHAPTER 2

2:1 Then Jonah prayed to the Lord his God out of the belly of the fish.

2:2 And he said, "I called to the Lord out of my trouble and He heard me; out of the belly of Sheol I cried and You listened to my voice."

2:3 "For You had hurled me into the depths, into the heart of the sea and the rivers surrounded me. All of your breakers and waves passed over me."

2:4 Then I said, "I am driven out of Your vision; yet, I will look again toward Your holy temple."

2:5 "The waters surrounded me, even to the soul; the deepness closed around me, the seaweeds were bound up around my head."

2:6 " I went down to the bottoms of the mountains; the land with her prison bars was around me forever; yet, You raised up my life from corruption, O Lord, my God."

2:7 "When my soul fainted within me, I remembered the Lord and my prayer came to You, into Your holy temple.

2:8 "They that keep false vanities forsake their own mercy."

2:9 "But I will sacrifice to You with the voice of thanksgiving; I will pay what I have vowed. Salvation is from the Lord.

2:10 And the Lord spoke to the fish and it vomited up Jonah upon the dry land.

CHAPTER 3

3:1 And the word of the Lord came to Jonah the second time, saying,

3:2 "Rise up, go to Nineveh, that great city, and call out to it the proclamation that I speak."

3:3 So Jonah arose and went to Nineveh, according to the Word of the Lord. Now Nineveh was an exceedingly great city of a three days walk.

3:4 And Jonah came into the city one day's walk and he called out and said, "Yet forty days and Nineveh will be overthrown."

3:5 So the people of Nineveh believed in God and called for a fast and put on sackcloth, from the greatest of them to the least of them.

3:6 Now word of it came to the king of Nineveh and he rose up from his throne and he laid aside his robe from himself and he covered himself with sackcloth and he sat in ashes.

3:7 And it was proclaimed and spoken throughout Nineveh by the decree of the King and his Nobles saying, "Let neither man nor beast, cattle nor flock, taste anything. Let them not feed nor drink water."

3:8 "But let man and beast be covered with sackcloth and cry out with great might to God; Yes, let them turn everyone from his evil ways and from the cruelty that is in their hands."

3:9 "Who can tell if God will back off and pity us and turn away from His burning anger, that we do not perish."

3:10 And God looked upon their doings, that they turned back from their evil course of life and God was sorry about the disaster that He had declared that He would bring upon them; and He did not do it.

CHAPTER 4

4:1 But it grieved Jonah greatly, and he was burned up with anger.

4:2 And he prayed to the Lord and said, "Ah now, I pray You, God. Did I not say so, when I was still on my soil? Therefore I fled to Tarshish; for I was aware that You are a gracious God, and compassionate, slow to become angry, and of abundant kindness, and are sorry about the disaster."

4:3 "Therefore now, O Lord, take, I ask You, my breath from me, for it is better for me to die than to be alive."

4:4 The Lord answered, "Does it seem best for you to be incensed?"

4:5 So Jonah went out of the city and sat eastward from the city, made himself a booth, and sat under it in the shade, until he could see what would happen to the city.

4:6 And God appointed a gourd and made it to grow high over Jonah, that it might be shade over his head, to deliver him from his distress. So Jonah was very cheered up by the gourd.

4:7 But God appointed a worm when morning broke the next day and it damaged the gourd so that it withered.

4:8 And it happened, when the sun arose, that God appointed a sultry east wind and the sun beat upon the head of Jonah so that he fainted. He begged within himself to die and he said, "It is best for me to die, rather than to live."

4:9 And God asked Jonah, "Do you do right to be incensed about the gourd?" And he answered, "I do right to be incense, enough to die."

4:10 Then the Lord said, "You had compassion on the gourd, for which you did not labor, neither made it grow up; which came up in a night and perished in a night."

4:11 "And should I not pity Nineveh, that great city, wherein there exist more than one hundred and twenty thousand persons who cannot discern between their right hand and their left hand, and also abundant cattle?"

THE BOOK OF JONAH

JONAH: THE RUNAWAY PROPHET

INTRODUCTION

The Book of Jonah has always been somewhat of a puzzle to theologians and others who study the Holy Scriptures. Serious questions seem to arise on almost every page. For example, is it really an historical account, or is it a fictional account with a moral to be recognized, or is it a rollicking tale that was told by Israeli sheepherders around a nighttime campfire? Is it an actual account of one man's struggle with God, or is it an allegory or even a parable such as Jesus told in the days of his earthly ministry? To say the least, it is a captivating story which draws us into itself. It is a story of sin, repentance and the wonderful grace of God. It is our story as well as Jonah's.

The Jewish people read this book in its entirety in their synagogues on Yom Kippur, the Day of Atonement, because it speaks of forgiveness and grace. On that day Jews ask one another for forgiveness. From ancient times the Jews have believed that if one cannot forgive a friend, he can also not expect forgiveness from God.

We, as Christians, also carry out this conviction. In the Lord's Prayer, Christians pray "forgive us our trespasses as we forgive those who trespass against us." Simply put, we are forgiven as much as we are willing to forgive others.

In these brief studies we will attempt to go along with Jonah as he tries to flee from God, only to find that, in the end, he is not able to do so. We will try to understand what this reluctant prophet is thinking as he digs in his heels to try to resist God.

It is our story as well and we will also see how God is awesomely successful in heathen Nineveh in spite of Jonah's stubbornness. No matter what Jonah does or tries to do on his own, it is God who is always in control and in charge.

The overwhelming question with which we begin is: Why is God sending a Jewish missionary to preach to the heathen gentiles of Nineveh? The answer, of course, is God's grace and His unending love. It is God's will that all men should be save (I Tim. 2:4, NKJV). All men are brothers because God, our Creator, is also our Father. His grace is shown in unending mercy. God's grace and His love for the sinful people of Nineveh is the theme of the book.

"Grace," in the Holy Scriptures, is undeserved mercy and loving kindness. In Gen. 6:8 (NKJV), Noah found grace in the sight of God. Perhaps one of the greatest examples of grace is recorded in the Book of Judges. In Judges 7:1-22 (NKJV), God shows Gideon how powerful grace really is. It does not take us long to notice that the most powerful theme of the whole Book of Jonah is God's eternal grace to sinful people.

It is interesting to note here that Jonah is also the only Old Testament prophet whom God sent as a missionary to heathen people with a message. He is charged to preach the message that God is sovereign and that He requires genuine repentance.

CHAPTER 1

"NOT ME, LORD"
JONAH 1:1-2

Jonah, a Jewish Prophet of God, is commanded by God to go to Nineveh, the capital city of Assyria, to preach to those sinful people. It is about the year 750 B.C. and to Jonah it is rather strange command, since the Assyrians are Gentiles (a Gentile is anyone who is not Jewish) and they and the Israelites have always been the very bitterest of enemies. Also, the Assyrians were such an aggressive warrior nation that the very thought of going there to preach to them repulses Jonah. He decides that he will not heed God's call and he will not go to Nineveh under any circumstances. After all, why should he preach God's salvation to one of Israel's fiercest enemies? Why should he care about them, anyway? And why in the world was God so concerned about them? Besides it could even cost Jonah his life to go there!

Nineveh is first mentioned in Genesis 10:11(NKJV) where Nimrod, a Cushite, a mighty hunter and ruler (i.e. an Ethiopian, and the great-grandson of Noah), went into Assyria and founded Babylon and Nineveh. (Gen. 10:8-11, NKJV). He also built the Tower of Babel and led many people to rebel against God. It is not mentioned again until the time of Jonah, in the eighth century, when it is described as being a "great and powerful city" and, apparently, the capital city of the Assyrian Empire (II Kings 19:36 NKJV). It was also a great center for the worship of Ishtar (Astarte), the fertility goddess. In Jonah's time, Nineveh was probably the greatest city in the world. But like most of the ancient cities which sooner or later declined in power, Nahum the Prophet writes: "Wasted is Nineveh; who will bemoan her?" (Nahum 3:7 NKJV), as he consigns the city to a pile of trash. Nahum also preached to Nineveh, but without the success which Jonah accomplished in that city.

Nineveh lay on the eastern bank of the Tigris River. Today it lies about 280 miles north of Babylon, opposite the city of Mosul (which was the hometown of the late dictator, Saddam Hussein), and which today is in the nation of Iraq. Though it became one of the great ancient cities, it was totally laid waste by the enemy armies of the Babylonians, the Medes and the Scythians about 612 BCE. For almost two and a half millennia, it was little more than a name. There was scarcely more than a pile of dust to identify it. In fact, some early scholars even theorized that perhaps the city had never existed at all. Three hundred years later, the troops of Alexander the Great could not even find anything to show where the city had been.

Excavations by archaeologists in recent years have uncovered palaces, works of art, inscriptions, sculpted figures and perhaps the most remarkable of all—the library of King Ashurbanipal, who reigned from 669-626 B.C.E. His library contained about ten thousand tablets, written in Assyrian, and contains a record of the history, religion and laws of Assyria. However, no mention of Jonah is found in any Assyrian literature. This is not so unusual, however, since there are also no secular records to indicate that Abraham, Isaac, Jacob, or Moses or Joseph ever existed. All we have are the Scriptural records. Other documents in the library collection, however, are believe to date back to the time of Abraham.

It might be noted here that the Assyrians were very inventive people. From them comes the inventing of paved roads, the invention of locks and keys, they devised the first postal system, they invented plumbing and the flush toilet, they devised a method of keeping time, they discovered ways of using iron, they invented libraries, and they had the first territorial divisions of land with regional governors. It should be noted that the Assyrians were some of the first Christian converts and they became a powerful Christian community which sent missionaries. Today the ancient city of Nineveh has been covered over by a new city, Nebi Yunis ("the Prophet Jonah"). The people who live there believe that Jonah is buried in Nebi Yunis. With tongue in cheek, the people tell a story. There are two mounds of earth in modern Nineveh. The smaller of the two is believed to be the grave of Jonah. The larger mound, they say, is where the great fish which swallowed Jonah is buried.

The legend is that the people of Nineveh carried the great fish up the river to the city and buried it in that place.

NEWS FLASH!!! On July 24, 2014 the news from the Middle East reported that the tomb of Jonah, in Nebi Yunis, near the Iraq city of Mosul, had been completely destroyed by the Islamic State terrorist group made up of Sunni terrorist Muslims. The Sunni Muslims ordered the people in the area to stay away from the shrine and they then closed the roads. It took the terrorists an hour to rig the shrine with explosives.

In related news, we have also been informed that the museum of the city of Mosul has been razed and artifacts dating to before 2,000 B.C. have been destroyed. This was accomplished on February 25-28, 2015.

The ISIS group established a "caliphate" and has destroyed most of the 3,000 year old city of Nimrod and they have also bulldozed the 2,000 year old city of Hatra —both of which are UNESCO sites. In their path of destruction, Walid and Theodore of Shoebat. com report that they also torched eleven churches and monasteries in the city of Mosul, as well as statues of poets, and people who were famous in their history.

Three Sunni clerics were also murdered by the ISIS in different parts of Mosul.

An Iraqi official said the destruction of Nebi Junis, the Tomb of Jonah, suffered the most damage of all the shrines which they destroyed in Iraq. The entire shrine and the tomb of the Prophet was reduced to dust. In addition, they also destroyed the shrine of the prophet Shayth (Seth) which was inside the city of Mosul.

The Islamic State group is trying to create a society as it was in its former days of Islam. They are feared by the local people because they are regarded as heretics and so they are in danger of being put to death.

There are also two palace mounds. These were the sites of the palaces of King Sennacherib and King Ashurbanipal. There is also a smaller mound which served as a military barracks. On this mound is where the Mosque of Jonah is now located.

Why did ISIS choose to do this? Mark Movsesian writes that most scholars and commentators believe that this is part of ISIS. One of the greatest difficulties that we encounter in our study of the Book of Jonah is the size of the city of Ninevah. It is described as being "a great and powerful city" and that it was "an exceedingly great city of three days journey" (3:3). Whatever does this mean?

An ancient historian tells us that the city formed a quadrangle which was surrounded by walls one hundred feet high, with the thickness of three chariots. The wall had fifteen hundred towers rising to a height of two hundred feet. Within the Book of Jonah we also learn that it was a city "of three days journey" and that it had a population of "more than one hundred and twenty thousand persons who could not discern between their right hand and left hand, and also abundant cattle" (Jonah 4:11, WHW). If we accept this, we must remember that the Jewish "days journey" was regarded as being twenty miles, leading us to believe that either the writer was exaggerating, or that the description also included the entire surrounding area, not included within the city walls. Perhaps the "three days journey" referred to the city in circuit, thereby giving it a circumference of sixty miles.

Jonah, whose name means "dove," was the son of Amittai. According to the ancient Jewish rabbis, they say that he was also the son of the widow at Zaraphath (I Kings

17:8-24 NKJV), or, even the son of the Shunammite woman whom Elisha raised from the dead (II Kings 4:32-37 NKJV). However, these traditions are highly doubtful and cannot be proved. He was from Gath-hepher, a town in Lower Galilee, in that section of land which was allotted to Jacob's tenth son, Zebulun (Gen. 49:13 NKJV), when the Israelites entered the land of Canaan after the exodus from Egypt. The Jewish Talmud also says that his father was from the Tribe of Zebulun and his mother was from the Tribe of Asher. The town was also about three miles northeast of Nazareth, the hometown of Jesus.

The tomb of Jonah is supposedly located both at Gath-hepher, his hometown, and also at Nineveh, which is not so unusual for prominent biblical figures in the Holy Land. Many of the most famous biblical figures are reportedly buried in several places. Today, the most recent archaeological findings are that Jonah is also possibly buried at the Hill of Jonah (Giv'at Yonah) at Ashdod, or possibly in Talpiot, a neighborhood of Jerusalem less than two miles south of the Old City. An ossuary, or "bone box" was discovered and there is some carving on the ossuary showing a large fish with a stick figure in its mouth. The date of the ossuary is from the period of 20 BCE until approximately 70 CE. Whether this stick figure is a person (Jonah?), or some Hebrew letters, or something else, is unknown. The inscription is unclear.

Approximately 2,000 ossuaries have been recovered by the Israel Antiquities Authority. Not all of them, (only about 650) have inscriptions inscribed upon them. Even so, most of these inscriptions are a warning to not disturb the bones of the dead.

James Tabor, an archaeologist and professor of religious studies at the University of North Carolina has noted that on one side of the box is the tail of a fish disappearing off the edge, as if it was diving into the water. There are also other smaller fish and a gate which the professor sees as the entrance to the "bars of death" mentioned in the Book of Jonah (Jonah 2:6 WHW).

Legend has it that Jonah did not remain in Israel after this because the Jews were jealous of him. Jonah was afraid because he had prophesied and his prophecy had not come true. It is said that he took his mother and returned to Judea. His mother died on the way and he buried her next to the Prophetess Deborah. He lived in the land of Serida and died two years after the people returned from Babylon. He was buried in the cave of Kainan.

Of Jonah's family and background we are told almost nothing, but the general consensus among scholars seems to be, that, in the line of the Prophets, Jonah comes after Elijah and Elisha. Some scholars also feel that Jonah was also a student of Elisha, the Prophet.

Rabbinic tradition says that a woman of Shunem regularly fed and gave shelter to Elisha when he passed that way. This woman was old and she had not had a son. Elisha made a prophecy that she would still bear a son, even in her old age. The prophecy came true and the boy grew into a man. One day he developed a severe headache (II Kings 4:19 NKJV). The boy died, but Elisha raised him to life. According to Jewish tradition, that boy was Jonah. Again, it is only legend.

Note here, that in the Book of Jonah, Jonah is never officially referred to as a prophet. And, as Elie Wiesel, the great Jewish writer and philosopher writes, he "entertains more than he disturbs." But he also makes us think deeply about sin, repentance, and grace. Jonah also lived in the time of the biblical Prophets Amos and Hosea.

There are those, in liberal theology, who try to prove that Jonah never existed at all. However, in the New Testament, Jesus referred to him as an actual person who preached in the city of Nineveh. In Matthew 12:39-41 (NRSV) we read:

"But He answered them, 'An evil and adulterous generation asks for a sign, but no sign will be given to it except the sign of the prophet Jonah. For as Jonah was three days and three nights in the belly of the sea monster, so for three days and three nights the Son of Man will be in the heart of the earth. The people of Nineveh will rise up at the judgement with this generation and condemn it, because they repented at the proclamation of Jonah; and see, something greater than Jonah is here!'"

And in Luke 11:29-32 (NRSV) we read:

"When the crowds were increasing, He began to say, 'This generation is an evil generation; it asks for a sign, but no sign will be given to it except the sign of Jonah. For as Jonah became a sign to the people of Nineveh, so the Son of Man will be to this generation. The queen of the South will rise at the judgement with the people of this generation and condemn them, because she came from the ends of the earth, to listen to the wisdom of Solomon, and see, something greater than Solomon is here. The people of Nineveh will rise up at the judgement with this generation and condemn it, because they repented at the proclamation of Jonah, and see, something greater than Jonah is here!'"

To us, as Christians in New Testament times, the "Sign of Jonah" is, of course, an image of Christ's dying and rising again on the third day. It was a warning to sinful Israel, in Old Testament times, that even nasty and heathen repented when Jonah preached. The people of Israel are here warned that they are in great spiritual danger of rejecting the one who is "greater than Jonah, that is," Jesus, the Messiah.

Jonah was a prophet, that is, he was the mouthpiece of God to His people. A prophet is "one who speaks for another" with the message: "Thus says the Lord." He tells, shares and proclaims the "good news" of God and His love and grace to all people. His prophetic obligation was total obedience and his work as a prophet was to preach and teach, and only incidentally to look into the future. He very likely prophesied during the reign of King Jeroboam, about 750 BCE. It reminds us of St. Paul, who said, "How can they know unless they are told?" It shows us the importance of preaching. Preaching the Word of God is actually the proclaiming of a means of grace. An interesting and frightening thought comes to mind now—what if Jonah, as a human being, had gone to express his own opinions to the Assyrians?

God wanted Jonah to go to Nineveh and to preach to them. But why was that so important? God said, "Because their evil has come up before Me" (Jonah 1:2, WHW). Their sins had become unbearable to God.

Jonah was to go and proclaim a verdict of death to the people of Nineveh. Perhaps it was not a convenient time for Jonah to go to Nineveh, but we need to remember that God calls for our obedience even when it may not be convenient for any of us to enter into His service.

Nowhere are we told what Nineveh's "evil" was, but the Hebrew word which is used in the book of Jonah suggests that it was violence or lawlessness. This would also be consistent with the fact that Assyria was such a ferocious enemy of Israel. The Assyrians were certainly well known for their cruelty and torture. Assyrian kings even boasted about how badly they dealt with their prisoners of war. They would gouge out eyes and cut out tongues and cut off noses. They would skin prisoners' bodies and leave them to dry in the hot sun. They tied groups of prisoners together and drove them into the hot desert to die, and they also ran poles through the bodies of their prisoners or dropped them into a deep pit and sealed it shut.

But now, the questions that arise for us are: "Will Jonah answer God's call?" "With what language will he speak to them?" "What authority will he have?" and, "Why does God want to send a Hebrew missionary to preach to the people in hard-hearted and Gentile Nineveh?" What should Jonah expect from his preaching to Nineveh? What evils should the Christian church be preaching against today?

Chapter 2

"A PROPHET WHO REFUSES HIS CALL"
JONAH 1:3-9

Jonah was a prophet of God, and to this very human person, God spoke and said, "Arise, go to Nineveh, that powerful city, and call out (to them) that their evil has come up before Me" (Jonah 1:2, WHW). The story is almost a mystery story.

Jonah is to preach to the Ninevites. The way that God speaks to him, it seems to indicate that Jonah was surely not a beginner as a prophet.

Isn't it interesting to note here that to almost all of the Prophets God said, "Arise"? Were they always just sitting around and waiting for something to happen? Surely, if this were the case, Jonah would much have preferred to remain seated in this event! But, God wanted him to "arise" and go to "Nineveh, that great city" and preach. His message was to be simple enough— "Their evil has come up before Me." In other words, if they didn't shape up spiritually, God was going to destroy them! Think about Sodom and Gomorrah for a moment. God didn't even send a preacher to warn them! (Gen. 18:16-19:29 NRSV). The Lord appeared to Abraham in his tent and he was told that the cities of Sodom and Gomorrah were going to be destroyed the next day. But even though the Lord and his two angels went to the wicked cities, no preaching took place before their destruction.

It was very confusing. "What is going on here anyway?" Jonah seems to ask this question when he complains to God. The plot of the Book of Jonah now seems to be taking shape. This is probably not Jonah's first mission, but it does not seem that Jonah took a very long time to come to a decision about what he was going to do.

He was not going to Nineveh and he was definitely not going to do anything to try to save those people in Nineveh. God must be joking and Jonah's decision was final!

Jonah wanted nothing whatsoever to do with Nineveh! After all, the Ninevites were Israel's longtime enemy! Why should he even care if they were saved or not? Jonah reasoned that the Ninevites surely did not deserve God's mercy and salvation. And besides that, did God really want to save Assyria so that it could later turn around and destroy Israel (which it actually did a few decades later)! No way! Jonah probably wanted Nineveh to suffer the same terrible judgement and fate which God had brought upon the cities of Sodom and Gomorrah. As we have said, it probably was not Jonah's first mission, but it very likely was his first refusal to do God's command. But what kind of God's prophet would not want people to be saved?

What could Jonah do? He couldn't stay where he was because God wouldn't give him any rest in that place. God knew where he was in Israel—and so he had to escape, anywhere, away from God, to somewhere else. He had to get out of Israel to get away from

God. Along with his fellow countrymen Jonah firmly believed that God was only in Israel with His chosen people, and nowhere else. People in each land believed that they had their own god(s). He had to get out of Israel now! He had to somehow hide from the God of Israel and hope that God would eventually forget about Nineveh or else ask someone else to go and proclaim His message. The lesson here is that just being a part of "Israel" does not make one righteous. At this point, Jonah gave more thought to his own sense of honor and safety than he did to God's love and glory and mercy for His people.

What options did Jonah really have? He could stay and suffer the consequences for his disobedience to God, or he could run away to a place where God would not be able to find him. The latter seemed like the most logical thing for him to do. He forgot that though man can run away from man, no one can run away from God!

The harbor at Joppa (today it is called Jaffa, on the Mediterranean coast of Israel, near to Tel Aviv) was a busy place, with ships and boats arriving and departing daily for many parts of the world. Surely, Jonah would be able to find a ship in this harbor which could carry him away from Israel, and even more important, away from God. It had to be a distant land, but, of course, Jonah had no idea at the moment where that might be. He had to find out where the ships in the harbor were headed.

Still, his basic problem at the point is: "…for I was aware that You are a gracious God, and compassionate, slow (patient) to become angry, and of abundant kindness, and are sorry about the disaster" (Jonah 4:2 WHW). In the Old Testament the prevalent idea among the Jews was—you get what you deserve. But now, a new theory was arising in Jewish theology. And it was: If you repented of your sins, you could receive forgiveness and not receive God's punishment for sin. It was something that Jonah could neither understand nor accept.

With his sack of worldly possessions in hand, Jonah now began to inquire where the ships in Jaffa were headed. Where would he go? North, south, or west? Where could he best get away and hide from God?

Jonah soon found his answer. He "found a ship going to Tarshish" (Jonah 1:3, WHW). When he was told by

God to go east to Nineveh, he found a boat that was going where he wanted to go—to the opposite direction, to the west (Jonah 1:3, WHW)! It was headed toward Spain. It was exactly what he wanted! Spain was in the opposite direction of Nineveh! And, according to Jewish belief, God would not be there. God was only in Israel. However, Jonah forgot something. God didn't choose Israel to be the "chosen people" because they were so good or so large. He chose them out of His love and grace. But Jonah was not showing that same love to the Ninevites and he certainly wasn't being gracious. He was being a totally sinful human being—stubborn, mean and hateful and self-centered. And so it was, then, that Jonah paid the fare and he went down into the hold of the ship to hide from God.

The harbor and city of Jaffa has a legendary history. The name "Jaffa" or "Joppa" as it was called in those days, means "beauty" in Hebrew. Old biblical legend says that the town was founded right after the Great Flood by Japheth, the son of Noah, who named the city after himself.

Joppa was attacked by the Pharaoh Thutmose III of Egypt in the year 1440 BCE. In a very interesting trick,

Thutmose's general Djehuty had two hundred sealed baskets, supposedly filled with grain, delivered into the city. When all the baskets had been brought in, the Egyptians soldiers jumped out of the baskets and defeated the city. It makes one think about the city of Troy and the wooden horse!

Jaffa was later destroyed by the Emperor Napoleon in 1799. The monastery and St. Peter's church in Jaffa are reported to stand on the very place where Napoleon and his troops camped. The ship left the harbor and almost immediately, after reaching the high seas, God "hurled a mighty wind into the sea and there was a great storm in the sea, so that the ship was thinking about breaking up (into) pieces" (Jonah 1:4, WHW).

When we think about miracles, we usually think about the New Testament and about the miracles of Jesus. The miracles of healing, of raising the dead, of walking on water and of feeding great groups of people are ascribed to Jesus, whose very being was filled with love and compassion for people. but, we must not forget that there were also countless miracles in the Old Testament. The crossing of the Red Sea (really, the "Reed Sea") by Moses and the people of

Israel (Exodus 14 NSRV), the ascension into heaven by the Prophet Elijah with the whirlwind and the fiery chariot (II Kings 2:11-12 NRSV), and the healing miracles done by the Prophet Elisha (II Kings 2:7 NRSV) are but a few of them. And the Book of Jonah literally has miracles in every chapter. Here, then, is miracle number one, with God ordering a huge storm that was strong enough to destroy the ship and everyone on board. To be sure, it is a tragic scene, with the ship being tossed about like a toy boat in a bathtub and the helpless sailors unable to do a thing about it.

The writer of the Book of Jonah, whether it be Jonah or someone else, does have a sense of humor. In something that we call a "personification" or an "anthropomorphism," he ascribes human attributes to the ship! The Hebrew text says that the ship was "thinking about breaking up into pieces" (Jonah 1:4, WHW), something which is not usually found in our English translations. Even the ship's feelings now become a part of the struggle for survival! The book also says that Jonah paid "her fare", giving gender to the ship.

The sailors were good-natured heathens, probably most of them Phoenicians, who now cried out, "…every man of them to his god" (Jonah 1:5, WHW). Very likely they called out to the heathen gods Ba'al and Ashtoreth and the whole host of other gods. If foxholes and war make believers out of the most callous men, so do storms at sea when the ship is on the verge of capsizing.

Apparently it was the worst storm that any of the sailors had ever experienced. They needed all the help they could summon. The sailors reasoned that the more gods they could make happy, the better chance they had of surviving the storm. They prayed to their own gods, but they received no answer. Perhaps it was because those gods were idols and they weren't really there! They even threw the ship's cargo into the sea to make the vessel lighter. But to no avail! The ship was surely doomed to capsize and sink into the depths of the sea.

Now, where was Jonah in the midst of all of this? was he helping to dump the cargo, or was he seasick and leaning over the rail of the ship? Actually, he had gone down inside of the ship and he was sound asleep (Jonah 1:5, WHW)! It brings to mind the Disciples in the Garden of Gethsemane. He should have been watching and praying. Jonah could relax because he smugly thought he had outsmarted God, and that he had moved out of God's reach. He was oblivious to the storm, the danger, and even to the plight of everyone else on board. He was insensitive to everyone, including God. Dr. Martin Luther humorously said, "Er schnarcht in seine Suenden", that is, "He snores in his sins."

The sailors struggle desperately to keep the ship afloat, but they seem to be fighting a losing battle. They pray to their heathen gods, but of course, no one is listening. The ship is about to break up and they have nothing more to try.

Even the captain (the Hebrew refers to him as the "chief rope puller" or the "chief knot-tier"), pagan but pious, is frantic at this point and he goes down into the hold of the ship and confronts his strange passenger with the words, "What do you mean, O sleeper? Arise, cry out to your God, so that God will think of us, so that we do not perish" (Jonah 1:6, WHW). Really what he is saying to Jonah is, "Right now, pray because we need all the help we can get!" This is a reminder to us that the Bible is the story of God's great search for man—from looking for Adam who was hiding from God in the Garden of Eden to the Book of Revelation where Christ says, "Behold, I stand at the door and knock" (Rev. 3:20 NRSV). God is here dramatically trying to get Jonah's attention!

In the meantime, however, the sailors are totally confused. They ask, "Why is this happening to us anyway? Who is to blame for all of this?" Truly, it must be someone on board, and so, they decide to cast lots to see who is at fault here (Jonah 1:7, WHW), a method which was widely used in biblical times. It can be compared to our practice of drawing straws. The soldiers at the Cross of Jesus also cast lots for His robe. To replace Judas, the Disciples cast lots and chose Mathias. Many years before, even the land of Canaan was divided among the people of Israel by lot (Num. 26:25 NRSV). But here, on the raging sea, the sailors were sure that someone on board the ship must be at fault!

Now, isn't this just amazing? The "lot fell on Jonah" (Jonah 1:7, WHW). And so the sailors now confront him and ask, "Make known to us, for whose cause this evil is upon us; what is your work? And from where do you come? What is your land and from what people are you?" (Jonah 1:8, WHW). They question his heritage and, in effect, they are asking him, "Who is your father?" and "What is your religion?" A side note here: Today one proves his Israeli heritage from his mother. One cannot prove who his father is. From here on, Jonah knows full well now that God is aware of where his location is. And with this, he is forced to confess, "I am a Hebrew; and I fear (worship) the Lord, the God of the heavens, who has made the sea and the dry land" (Jonah 1:9, WHW). In all honesty, Jonah should really have said, "I used to worship" God.

Somehow, it just doesn't tie in—for if God made heaven and earth, how can Jonah ever expect to escape from Him? It was sheer pride and nonsense on his part. Everything belonged to God! God cannot and will not be avoided.

Jonah admits his failure and confesses, "I am a Jew."

CHAPTER 3

"JONAH'S DAY OF RECKONING"
JONAH 1:10-17

The sailors were terrified and they asked Jonah, "Why have you done this? For the men now perceived that he had fled from the face of the Lord..." (Jonah 1:10, WHW). The sailors were amazed and bewildered that Jonah would dare to displease his God so much. They scold him and tell him to pray to his God. The sailors are actually here preaching to Jonah! "What shall we do to you, that the sea may be quiet for us?" (Jonah 1:11, WHW). The suspense begins to mount and now we are given questions which we cannot answer.

The sailors, who had spent so much of their lives trying to pacify their heathen gods, came to the conclusion that Jonah must be running away from a much more powerful God than they had ever known. With every passing moment, the sea is growing more and more stormy and the ship is about to capsize. Now Jonah knows full well what the difficulty is, and so he announces the only solution that he knows to solve it. He says, "Lift me up and cast me away into the sea; then shall the sea be quiet for you" (Jonah 1:12 WHW). Jonah knows that the storm is raging on his account, but now he also feels a sense of justice, fairness and rightness. He is willing to die for his sins. God is angry and Jonah feels that His anger will only subside when he is destroyed. He asks the sailors now to toss him overboard (Jonah 1:12,WHW). A question now arises: Why didn't Jonah just end his own life by jumping overboard? He probably didn't have the courage. But, he realizes that the sailors are suffering because of him and so now he is willing to die for his sins.

This willingness to die becomes a favorite "cop-out" for Jonah. However, this is the first time he mentions it. He will suggest it twice more before the book ends. It seems to be a simple solution for him to end all of his problems.

And yet, even with his death-wish, he always wants his life to go on!

The good-hearted heathen sailors, however, are considerably more compassionate here than their Jewish passenger. They feel that somehow Jonah must be a very important person to have such a mighty God raging such a strong storm against him. He must be a really valuable servant of God to create such a scene and so they use all of their strength to try to row the ship toward shore, but despite their best efforts, they cannot do it (Jonah 1:13, WHW). The ship is doomed to capsize. All of them are facing certain death. And the storm is not ceasing its raging.

The sailors, who have already given up praying to their own false gods, now turn their beliefs to Jonah's true God and they cry out to Him, "We ask you, O Lord, do not let us perish for this man's (soul) life, and do not lay upon us innocent blood; for you, O Lord, have done as it has pleased you" (Jonah 1:14, WHW). The sailors, now believing in Jonah's God, the God who controls nature, are afraid of His anger and they do not want Jonah's death to be held against them if they die. Through the work of the Holy Spirit, the sailors here come to faith, which is God's second miracle in the book. We notice here with interest that Jonah does not pray with them in his plight. He cannot, for after all, he is running away from God and so he scarcely dares to pray to Him! If he were to pray to God, then God for sure would know where he was! Also, if God knew his whereabouts, would God even want to listen to him?

However, the awful moment has arrived. Nothing more can humanly be done and so the sailors pick up Jonah and toss him into the sea. This was perhaps somewhat selfish on their part, since it really was their obligation to protect their paying passenger. Why should they live and Jonah die, even though tossing him into the sea was Jonah's idea. And immediately the storm was calmed (Jonah 1:15. WHW). It was absolutely amazing! Notice now that the sailors "were greatly afraid of the Lord and they offered a sacrifice to the Lord, and they made vows to Him (Jonah 1:16,

WHW)". They now pray to Jonah's God! They beg for His pardon for what they had to do. They were not about to take any unnecessary chances with such a powerful God! We are not sure of what the "sacrifice" was or what the "vows" they promised may have been, but they were probably vows that they would obey and serve Him. Also, they were vows which were made in great earnest.

But now, here comes the fantastic miracle of the "great fish" (Jonah 1:17, WHW), which is probably the most memorable part of the Book of Jonah. It is that part that most people remember best about the Jonah story. Another miracle takes place. "The Lord appointed a great fish to swallow Jonah. A Jewish Midrash says that "Jonah entered the mouth of the whale (?) as one enters a synagogue." And Jonah was in the belly of the fish three days and three nights" (Jonah 1:17, WHW). God has a way of bringing His servants to a speedy recognition of His will for them and of enforcing obedience to it.

The "three days" also remind us of the disciples who were on their way to the village of Emmaus on Easter Sunday afternoon (Luke 24:13-30 RSV). They were without hope because they had been sure that Jesus was going to redeem Israel. And now He was dead! Three days had passed since His death and they had run out of hope. They were about as hopeless as the sailors.

It is useless to conjecture what kind of fish it was. The Hebrew text does not say that it was a whale, but rather, a "great fish." Suffice it to say, this was a special miraculous fish which God prepared just for this moment. Even Jesus refers to this episode when He says, "For as Jonah was three days and three nights in the belly of a huge fish, so the Son of Man will be three days and three nights in the heart of the earth" (Matt. 12:39-40 RSV). After the time in the fish, Jonah was given life to preach to the people of Nineveh. When Jesus was given life by His Father, He rose from the three days and nights in the tomb and He sent His disciples into the world to preach the Gospel of salvation. Those who repented and believed were given the gift of eternal life.

An interesting thought: Why was Jonah so willing to give up his life?

CHAPTER 4

"I CRIED AND YOU LISTENED"
JONAH 2:1-4

One of the great miracles of Holy Scripture is presented in chapter two of the book of Jonah. Volumes have been written as writers have tried to determine what kind of "great fish" (Heb. dag gadol which refers to a number of sea creatures) swallowed Jonah. Many volumes have been written about how he could have possibly survived in the innards of the fish for three days and three nights and still have lived. How did he keep from being digested? The Old Testament refers to a huge mythical creature which they called "leviathan"

(Job 41:1,RSV; Isa. 27:1 RSV; etc.) Was the fish a "leviathan" or was the "fish" some sort of whale—as many children's writers seem to assume? In this book of miracles, it seems as if the "great fish" is really the least of our concerns. It's really only a "prop" in the drama of the book. God "assigned" or "appointed" or "prepared" a "great fish" created especially to carry out God's plan for Jonah and Nineveh. It's a special fish that carried Jonah to the depths of Sheol (Hebrew: hell) for three days and three nights. No other explanation is needed.

As this chapter begins, we have a lesson in prayer and we find Jonah praying a "psalm-like prayer" to the Lord his God from the bowels of the fish: (Jonah 2:1, WHW). It really becomes the theme of the whole book: "I called and You listened." Up until this time, Jonah has not uttered one word of prayer. Why? It was because he was running away from God! Would God even want to hear him now, or had God abandoned him to death? The suspense grows stronger as we wait for God's answer.

However, Jonah's need was now desperate and prayer appeared to be his last resort. He was drowning in despair and distress. But isn't this typical of all of us at one time or another in our lives? When do we pray? We also turn to prayer when there is seemingly no other way to turn, when we have reached our last resort, and when we are at the "end of our rope."

Prayer, for many of us, so often becomes little more than a hopeless cry to God in times of trouble. This is not as it should be. We ought to pray "first" instead of as a "last resort." God hears and God answers every prayer, and prayer increases our faith and our trust in God.

The fact that Jonah now prays to God is a fantastic surprise—really, another miracle, perhaps more fantastic than the wind or even the great fish. His prayer reminds us that God demands obedience and He is ready to give to those who repent. This opportunity is given here to Jonah and later on to the people of Nineveh.

What does Jonah pray? Some scholars have said that he is praying the words of a psalm which was extant in his day, but which has been lost to us today. The prayer is also reminiscent of Psalm 18:6 (NRSV):

In my distress I called upon the Lord,
and cried out to my God;
He heard my voice from His temple,
and my cry came before Him, even
to His ears.
and Psalm 30:4 (NRSV):
Sing praise to the Lord, you saints of His,
and give thanks at the remembrance of His holy name.

In any case, Jonah makes it very personal. He prays: "I called to the Lord out of my trouble and He heard me; out of the belly of Sheol (also used for the "underworld" or the "grave"). I cried and You listened to my voice" (Jonah 2:2, WHW). Jonah prays as if the Lord has already heard him and he prays as if God had already answered his prayer and delivered him from the belly of the fish. He prays, knowing that God had heard his prayers before and He will now hear them again. It is also the same way with us. He has heard and answered our prayers in the past, and He surely will hear us again.

Jonah continues to pray: "...You hurled me into the depths, into the midst of the sea and rivers surrounded me. All of Your breakers and Your waves passed over me" (Jonah 2:3, WHW). While Jonah was surely experiencing the movements of the sea inside of the fish, he suffered tremendous feelings of despair and guilt. He had committed terrible sins against God and he had acted foolishly before God and now he was face to face with death. He had miserably failed his God as a Prophet, but note that his prayer does not really show any sorrow over his sins. It does not even mention his disobedience to God.

Jonah continues, "I am driven out of Your vision; yet, I will look again toward Your holy temple" (Jonah 2:4, WHW). This is really a synonym for praying. Jonah remembers the wonderful days when he was in the Lord's Temple in Jerusalem. God had blessed him in so many ways. He remembers and he says that he will once again look toward God's holy temple. It is here that Jonah realizes, most of all, that he is an outcast, even from God. He knows now what it means to be alone— without God and without the temple.

This passage also speaks to our own church-going. When we are discouraged, it becomes very easy for us to neglect our church attendance. And yet, is it not in the church that you and I find refreshment and forgiveness and renewal for our souls? God hears and He will forgive our past deeds and sins and discouragements when we come to Him in repentance and prayer and worship.

In a desperate situation in our lives, why do we think about praying last, instead of first?

CHAPTER 5

"SALVATION IS FROM THE LORD"
JONAH 2:5-7

Jonah continues with his prayer from the belly of the great fish. His depression is expressed in everything he says.

Verses five and six are best read together. "The waters surrounded me, even to the soul: the deepness closed around me, the seaweeds were bound up around my head. I went down to the bottoms of the mountain; the land with her prison bars was around me forever: yet, you raised up my life from corruption, O Lord, my

God (Jonah 2:5-6, WHW). Notice here how Jonah describes his feelings of despondency; he says that he is "surrounded", "closed around", "bound up", "I went down", and "prison bars were around me forever." He is cut off from the living. Hope was fading quickly. Things seemed out of control, and he was not sure that he could "hang on" much longer. The weeds are wrapping themselves around him on the bottom of the sea and the abyss is rolling over him. There are mountains on the bottom of the sea and there is a door which leads to Sheol, a door which will close forever when he enters. Jonah compares the fish's belly to a tomb from which there is no escape. He feels as if he has joined the dead. Aren't those the feelings of a person who has also strayed away from God? Doesn't this also describe us as well as Jonah when we stray away from Him?

"When my soul was fainted within me, I remembered the Lord and my prayer came to You, into Your holy temple" (Jonah 2:7, WHW). When Jonah remembered God, he prayed and God heard him and caused something miraculous to happen. God spares Jonah's life, even though Jonah never confesses his own rebellion. It is sad, but there is no real indication that Jonah ever repented.

If we ever needed proof for the power of prayer, this truly is it. God was not yet through with Jonah, nor with his prophetic ministry. Jonah prays, "They that keep false vanities forsake their own mercy. But I will sacrifice to You the voice of thanksgiving; I will pay what I have vowed. Salvation (deliverance) is from the Lord" (Jonah 2:8-9, WHW). He says, "Those who depend upon themselves are not happy because they have refused to accept what God was willing to give them."

Jonah now makes a vow to God. True, it may have been a vow of desperation, but it was a vow that Jonah faithfully kep later on in his life. How many times have we, when a loved one was gravely ill, or in some other desperate situation, made vows to God only to forget all about them later when the danger had subsided?

"And the Lord spoke to the fish, and it vomited up Jonah upon the dry land." (Jonah 2:10, WHW). With these words, Jonah's adventure inside the great fish comes to a close. His life is spared because God is not through with him yet. Jonah had had a preview of hell, but God still has a mission for him to fulfill. God will not take "no" for an answer. The mission to Nineveh is still waiting for Jonah.

CHAPTER 6

"THE SECOND TIME AROUND"
JONAH 3:1-5

As we look at the opening sentence of chapter 3, we see that the Book of Jonah actually starts over. "And the word of the Lord came to Jonah the second time saying, "Rise up, go to Nineveh, that great city, and call out, tell, share and proclaim to it the proclamation that I speak" (Jonah 3:1-2, WHW).

This shows the importance of missionaries. Now there is even more anticipation than before! Repetition builds

suspense. What will Jonah do? God is here giving him a second chance.

This is the only time an Israeli prophet is sent to preach to people in a foreign country. "So Jonah arose and went to Nineveh, according to the word of God. Now Nineveh was an exceedingly great city of three days walk" (Jonah 3:3, WHW). (See the Introduction for Nineveh) This time, Jonah doesn't argue with God or try to run away again, but he now sets out to accomplish his mission to the city.

What wonderful patience God has with Jonah! In all of Scripture God is not portrayed more fair and generous than right here. God has chosen Jonah to do this task and it is what He wants Jonah to do. It also surely shows us a tremendous example of God's grace. It was undeserved mercy! Jonah certainly wasn't worthy, but God gave him a chance. Perhaps Jonah was not worthy to go to Nineveh, but the city had been ravaged by two plagues in 765 and 769 B.C.E. and a solar eclipse in 763 B.C.E., making the city ready to receive Jonah's message.

"And Jonah began to come into the city one day's walk, and he called and said, "Yet forty days and Nineveh will be overthrown" (Jonah 3:4, WHW). The missionaries task is to "tell", to "proclaim", and to "share." Surely, St. Paul speaks about this very thing in Romans 10:14-15a(NRSV).

He writes:

"How then shall they call on Him in
whom they have not believed? And
how shall they believe in Him of who
they have not heard? And how shall
they hear without a preacher? And
how shall they preach unless they are
sent?"

Between Jonah and St. Paul, we have definite charge from God to send missionaries to proclaim the good news of the Lord and of His salvation to those who have not heard.

The first thing that we note is that Jonah did not preach a message of salvation. It was only a message of warning. Also, it was not a cry against the sins of the city, as horrible as they were, but rather, it was an announcement of its overthrow in forty days. Whether this was the whole message or just the theme of his sermon, we are not told. Perhaps this was the most important part of his message. Whatever it was, it gave the people of Nineveh an opportunity to repent. It was the beginning of a forty day probation for the city. The Hebrew word for "overthrown" is the same word (Heb. haphak) that is used for Sodom and Gomorrah's destruction (Gen. 19:21, 25, 29 NRSV).

"So the people of Nineveh believed in God and called for a fast and to put on sackcloth, from the greatest of them to the least of them" (Jonah3:5, WHW). It was nothing short of fantastic! Has the Holy Spirit touched the hearts and souls of the Ninevites and was now doing the work of salvation in their lives? A great deal of controversy and speculation still exists among theologians as to whether the people had experienced a genuine conversion or not. Was it real, or was Jonah's pronouncement something resourceful that it frightened them to fear for their lives and so they converted?

The God of Israel was certainly an unknown being in the city of Nineveh. Perhaps theirs was a confession which only required them to listen to God's Word, to change their barbarous ways, and to look with hope to the future. Surely their repentance is another miracle of God. Jonah preached, but it was God who acted.

In biblical times, sackcloth was often worn as a sign of repentance and mourning. It is a rough and coarse material which, when worn next to the skin, was terribly uncomfortable and caused the skin to chafe and itch. It was worn to constantly remind a person of their sins and it was often used along with ashes and fasting.

CHAPTER 7

"A LESSON IN REPENTANCE"
JONAH 3:6-10

The King of Nineveh was quick to join his people, even though he probably had not heard Jonah preach. The text says: "Now word of it came to the King of Nineveh and he rose up from his throne and he put aside his robe, and he covered himself with sackcloth and he sat in ashes" (Jonah 3:6, WHW). The king cared a great deal for his people and he joined them in their penitence and in wearing the sackcloth. In addition, he also sat down in a pile of ashes to show his humility and to show that he was in mourning. The ashes, mixed with perspiration on the skin, formed a lye solution which painfully burned the person wearing it. It was semi-torture and a debasing of oneself. To endure it was a sign of sincere repentance.

We are not certain who the king of Nineveh was in Jonah's time. Governors of Nineveh held the office of King in Jonah's time, 789 and 761 BCE. Their names were Ninurta-mukin-ahi and Nabe-mukin-ahi respectively.

The king realized that much of the sin, wickedness and violence of Nineveh was really his responsibility. The repentance, by his decree, was to be complete, "...from the greatest to the least." And he and his nobles caused it to be proclaimed throughout Nineveh saying, "Let neither man nor beast, cattle nor flock, taste anything. Let them not feed nor drink water. But let man and beast be covered with sackcloth and cry out mightily to God; Yes, let everyone turn from his evil ways and from the cruelty that is in their hands. Who can tell if maybe God will back off and turn away from His burning anger, so that we do not perish" (Jonah 3:7-9, WHW)? It seems strange and sort of comical that it also included the cattle, but the decree from the king was really thorough. We also need to remember here that this repentance was not because of the size of the city, nor because the city was so "strong and powerful", but rather, that it was through the working of the Holy Spirit.

As we look at the Christian church today, it soon becomes evident that the church so often forgets its mission "from the greatest to the least." The poor are so often left behind and they suffer from a lack of recognition as God's children.

"And God looked upon their doings, that they turned back from their evil course of life and God was sorry about the calamity that He had declared that He would bring upon them; and He did not do it" (Jonah 3:10, WHW). Here we see another anthropomorphism, which is giving human attributes to God. God changes His mind. He will not destroy Nineveh. The people had responded to Him with repentance and a contrite heart.

How amazing! Here God shows His mercy to one of Israel's most hated enemies! Was this why Jonah didn't want to go to Nineveh? Did he surmise that God was so soft-hearted that he would not destroy Nineveh? Did he somehow know that God would change His mind? God loves all people, even the heathen and those whom we so often look down upon. The last thing Jonah wanted to see was the Ninevites being spared.

CHAPTER 8

"A LESSON IN COMPARISON"
JONAH 4

Chapter four of the Book of Jonah begins on a negative note. "It grieved Jonah greatly and he was very burned up (blazed) with anger" (Jonah 4:1, WHW). Jonah's life may have been spared, but he was not over his vengeful attitude. He still wanted Nineveh to be destroyed like Sodom and Gomorrah. His problem is still self-love and self-pity.

The Germans have a word for those who want to see bad things happen to their neighbor. That word is

"Schadenfreude", meaning that there is secret rejoicing if anything bad happens to them. How sad, when we think that Jonah should have rejoiced that God was feeling such compassion for Nineveh. God had also felt such tremendous mercy for Jonah; yet Jonah felt nothing of the kind for Nineveh. After such success, he is unhappy and even angry with God. Why isn't God happy just to be the God of the Jews? Was God even breaking the Covenant that He had made with Abraham?

"And he prayed to the Lord and said, "Ah now, I pray You, God, did I not say so when I was in my country? Therefore I fled to Tarshish: for I was aware that You are a gracious God and compassionate, patient to become angry, and of abundant kindness and are sorry about the calamity" (Jonah 4:2, WHW).

Jonah admits that he is prejudiced and also that he didn't really want God to show mercy to the people of Nineveh. He didn't want God to show any kindness toward them, but somehow, he just knew that God would! He feels that God is too easy. He just cannot get rid of the Jewish idea that gentiles are undeserving of God's blessing. He forgets that no one is too evil or too hopeless that God cannot reach down from heaven in mercy.

Here Jonah, once again, wants to die. He says, "Therefore now, O Lord, take, I ask You, my breath from me, for it is better for me to die than to be alive" (Jonah 4:3, WHW). Will his death be a great loss to the world and to God? Jonah does not approve of the way that God wants to do things, and so he wants to die. He wants to die, not because Nineveh did not listen—he wants to die because they did listen and they did obey. How pathetic! He would rather die than see Nineveh saved. In his failure to himself, he succeeds as God's servant. He fails as a runaway prophet and he even fails in his death wish.

We want God to act in certain ways in certain situations. The great author, C.S. Lewis, wrote about our putting "God in a Box." But as soon as we try to do this, God shows us that he is much bigger than that.

In verse 4 we read, "The Lord answered, 'Does it seem best to be incensed (upset, angry)? (Jonah 4:4, WHW). Does God need man to tell Him what to do? Should not the repentance of Nineveh qualify for God's mercy? Jonah feels that the whole thing is unfair, that God is much too easy. Even the immensity of God and His love doesn't appear to be enough for him in this case.

"So Jonah went out of the city and sat eastward from the city, made himself a booth (Heb. sukka) and sat under it in the shade, until he could see what would happen to the city" (Jonah 4:5, WHW). It appears that Jonah still harbors the hope that God will still destroy the city. The "booth" was probably similar to the ones which the Jews build for themselves on the Feast of Tabernacles. Also, he didn't want to be in the city if that judgement should still come. Isn't it easy to sit back and to wait on God's judgement upon others? It's so easy for us to become judgmental and to condemn others. And Jonah was angry, upset with God, and alone. He was not ready to see God's grace at work.

"And God appointed a gourd (Hebrew: kikayon) and made it to grow high (Heb. gadal) over Jonah, that is might be a shade over his head, to deliver him from his distress. So Jonah was very cheered up by the gourd" (Jonah 4:6, WHW). The plant becomes part of God's lesson to Jonah. God shows His mercy to

Jonah. He sends a vine, a gourd or castor oil plant, to grow above him and to shade him. God is again active in the world of nature. It was just as miraculous as the storm and the great fish. The Lord is loving and compassionate and He mercifully helps us to overcome whatever problem we are facing, even in the midst of our sinfulness.

"But God appointed a worm" when morning broke the next day and it wounded the gourd so that it withered and died. The plant and Jonah's joy over it is short lived. And it happened, when the sun arose, that God also appointed a sultry east wind and the sun beat upon the head of Jonah so that he fainted.

He begged within himself to die and he said, 'It is best for me to die, rather than to live'" (Jonah 4:7-8, WHW). This has gone far enough! It was time now to teach Jonah an important lesson. He needed to stop wallowing in self-pity and feeling sorry for himself and start thinking like a prophet. He needed to start thinking about others. Besides, he could have gone into the city and found relief. The Hebrew word is "ra'ah" which can be translated "discomfort", or even "evil" when it refers to the Ninevites' evil, and "displeased" when Jonah is upset that God will spare the city.

God sends a hot desert wind, commonly known as the Sirocco, and a hot scorching sun which beats on Jonah until he faints.

"During the period of a sirocco the temperature rises steeply, sometimes even climbing during the night, and it remains high, about 16-22 degrees above average... at times every scrap of moisture seems to have been extracted from the air, so that one has the curious feeling that one's skin has drawn much tighter than usual. Sirocco days are peculiarly trying to the temper and tend to make even the mildest people irritable and fretful and to snap at one another for apparently no reason at all.

He only seems to learn with painful visual aids.

Once again, God asks Jonah, "Do you do right to be incensed about the gourd?" And he answered, "I do right to be incensed; enough to die" (Jonah 4:9, WHW). Jonah was needing a serious course in anger management. He was wrong, although his anger and pride kept him from seeing it. It was as if he was telling God that He wasn't doing a very good job. He was still only interested in himself. He felt that God had taken away his dignity by not destroying Nineveh.

When Jonah asks to die, it reminds us of an incident in the life of Elijah (I Kings 19:1-4 NRSV). Elijah has just defeated the 450 prophets of Baal and the 400 prophets of Asherah and he had ordered all of them to be killed. When this was accomplished, Queen Jezebel, who supported the heathen prophets, gave the order to kill Elijah. He headed south to the desert to escape from Jezebel and when he was too hungry and tired to go on, he sat under a broom tree and also prayed to God to take his life.

It was time now for God to talk some sense to Jonah. Then the Lord said, "You had compassion on the gourd, for which you did not work, neither did you make it grow up; which came up in a night and perished in a night. And should I not spare Nineveh, that great city, wherein there are more than a hundred and twenty thousand persons who cannot discern between their right hand and their left hand, and also abundant cattle?" (Jonah 4:10-11, WHW). "You pitied the plant which you did not make, and you do not think that I should pity Nineveh (which I did make)?"

The lesson of this book hits home with full force. The last two verses contain the message that God wants Jonah to hear and digest. God does not only belong to Israel, but also to the Gentiles.

Jonah is concerned about a plant which grew up overnight and then died. But why isn't he concerned about the people of Nineveh? Aren't they more important than the gourd? There is no answer to God's last question. Jonah failed to love the people whom God had given to him.

The book doesn't end with a "happily ever after" conclusion. We are not told that Jonah ever repented nor that he even ended his stalemate with God. The book ends abruptly with the statement— "and also abundant cattle." Did Jonah have a change of heart? Did Nineveh continue to be a city of believers? History tells us that Nineveh soon fell into their old sinful ways again. Nahum the Prophet later went to preach to them, but they did not repent (as they did with Jonah). The city was finally destroyed by an alliance of the Babylonians, the Medes and the Scythians in 612 BCE.

Did Jonah finally get the point? The book closes without ever revealing Jonah's response to God, nor his repentance. However, this is not the point of the Book of Jonah. The question which God asks in verse 11 is one which each of us must answer. God teaches us a vital lesson in love. God loved the Ninevites and we should love people like them.

God is the real hero of the Book of Jonah. His control extends to nature, to the pagan Ninevites, and to the Prophet.

We do not really need to know the end of the book. Of much more importance is that the book is really about us too. It forces us to examine ourselves. But the book is not just about us—it is also addressed to all of Israel, which also rebelled against God again and again. It asks us and Israel, "Do we share God's concern?"

The ending sneaks up on us and is very subtle. It literally hits us over the head. And most important, it makes us think and draw our own conclusions.

What lessons do we learn from the Book of Jonah?

As we reflect on the book:

1) We learn about patience and the grace of God.

2) We see God's love and compassion when He gives Jonah a second chance.

3) We see how God answers prayer.

4) We see the omnipotent power of God at work in nature.

5) We see the power of the Holy Spirit at work in Jonah's preaching.

6. We see God's concern for all of mankind.

What did the Book of Jonah teach YOU?

RESOURCES

Baly, Dennis The Geography of the Bible

Beyer, Bryan and Walton, John. Obadiah, Jonah. (Grand Rapids, Michigan: Lamplighter Books. 1982).

Fairbarin, Patrick. Jonah. (Grand Rapids, Michigan: Kregel Publications. 1964).

Fretheim, Terence E. The Message of Jonah. (Minneapolis: Augsburg Publishing House. 1977).

Golka, Friedemann W. and Knight, George A.F. Revelation of God. (Grand Rapids: Wm. B. Eerdmanns Publishing Co. 1998)

Haller, Eduard. Die Erzaehlung von dem Propheten Jona. (Muenchen: Chr. Kaiser Verlag. 1958).

Hasel, Gerhard F. Jonah: Messenger of the Eleventh Hour. (Mountain View, California: Pacific Press Publishing Association. 1976).

Holy Bible. The New King James Version. (New York: American Bible Society. 1990). ((NRJV))

Holy Bible. The New Revised Standard Version. (Grand Rapids: Zondervan. 1989). ((NRSV))

Holy Bible. The New Revised Standard Version. (New York: Thomas Nelson Inc. 1972). ((RVS))

Person, Raymond F. In Conversation With Jonah. (Sheffield: Academic Press, Ltd. 1996).

Sasson, Jack M. The Anchor Bible, Jonah, Vol. 24. (New York: Doubleday. 1990).

Shepherd, David R. Editor-in-Chief, Jonah/Zephaniah. (Nashville, Tennessee: Broadman and Holman Publishers. 1999).

Simon, Uriel. Yonah. (Philadelphia: The Jewish Publication Society. 1999).

Smith, Billy K. Laymen's Bible Book Commentary, Vol. 13. (New York: Doubleday. 1990).

Spaude, Cyril W. People's Bible Book Commentary: Obadiah, Jonah, Micah. (Saint Louis: Concordia Publishing House. 1994).

Werner, Herbert. Jona: Der Mann aus dem Ghetto. (Goettingen: Vandenhoeck und Ruprecht, 1966).

Wiesel, Elie. Five Biblical Portraits (University of Notre Dame Press. 1981).

Winkler, Wilbert H. My own literal translation of the Book of Jonah from the original Hebrew. (WHW)

The copious notes were taken from the inspiring and insightful lectures by Dr. Herbert Leupold and Dr. Ronald Hals at Trinity Lutheran Seminary in Columbus, Ohio.

My eternal thanks!

NOTES

NOTES

NOTES

NOTES

NOTES

NOTES

NOTES

Printed in the United States
By Bookmasters